Cocos
Island

Welcome to Cocos Island! Once a haven for buccaneers, this exotic and remote island is still a destination for the adventurous.

DIVING AND SNORKELING GUIDE TO

Cocos Island

Lucy Agace

Pisces Books®
A division of Gulf Publishing Company
Houston, Texas

> **Publisher's note:** At the time of publication of this book, all the information was determined to be as accurate as possible. However, new construction may have changed land reference points, weather may have altered reef configurations, and some businesses may no longer be in operation. Your assistance in keeping future editions up-to-date will be greatly appreciated.
>
> Also, please pay particular attention to the diver rating system in this book. Know your limits!

Copyright © 1997 by Gulf Publishing Company, Houston, Texas. All rights reserved. This book, or parts thereof, may not be reproduced in any form without permission of the publisher.

Pisces Books®
A division of Gulf Publishing Company
P.O. Box 2608
Houston, Texas 77252-2608

Pisces Books is a registered trademark of Gulf Publishing Company.

Printed in Hong Kong

10 9 8 7 6 5 4 3 2 1

Library of Congress Cataloging-in-Publication Data
Agace, Lucy.
    Diving & snorkeling guide to Cocos Island / Lucy Agace.
      p. cm.
    Includes index.
    ISBN 1-55992-092-0
    1. Scuba diving—Costa Rica—Cocos Island—Guidebooks.
2. Skin diving—Costa Rica—Cocos Island—Guidebooks. 3. Cocos Island (Costa Rica)—Guidebooks. I. Title. II. Title: Diving and snorkeling guide to Cocos Island.
GV838.673.C8A43   1997
797.23'097286—DC21   96-37859
                                                            CIP

Table of Contents

How To Use This Guide — 1
  Rating System for Dives and Divers, 3

1 Overview of Cocos Island — 4
  Climate, 6 • Hiking, 8 • Geography, 10 • Accommodations, 11 • Cocos Marine Park, 11 • History and Treasure, 12

2 Diving in Cocos Island — 20
  Map of Dive Sites, 21
  Dirty Rock, 24
  Submerged Rock, 27
  Sharkfin Rock, 29
  Dos Amigos I, 31
  Dos Amigos II, 33
  Manuelita Island West, 35
  Manuelita Island East, 38
  Cousteau's Sea Mount, 42
  Manta Ray Point, 44
  Marble Ray Point, 48
  Chatham Bay, 52
  Wafer Bay, 56

3 Safe, Smart Diving — 58
  Reef Etiquette, 59 • Hazardous Marine Life, 61 • DAN, 62

Appendix—Diving Operations — 64

Index — 65

Acknowledgments

I would like to express my appreciation to a number of people, without whose support and enthusiasm this book could not have been completed.

First, to my husband, Jeremy, who discovered the extent of the magical, exhilarating diving this remote island has to offer. He prepared and researched our voyage and the eventual visit to Cocos Island surpassed our wildest dreams. We share a love of diving and exploring new places to dive, and over the years I have never met anyone who exceeds his passion and determination.

To Nicky Manwaring, who guided my writing hand.

To Sally Davies, Robert Bryning, Hernan Vargas, and the crew of *Ocean Trilogy*—Captain Andy Fletcher, Graham Towers, Gay Taffe, Vicky Ferguson, and Stacy.

A blenny plays "peek-a-boo" on a Cocos Island reef.

How To Use This Guide

This guide is designed to prepare you for your visit to Cocos Island. The majority of readers will be diving from live-aboard boats and so will not need to find dive sites themselves. However, this guide will acquaint you with each dive, including information on currents, depths, photo hints, and underwater topography. The average live-aboard trip is 10–14 days, so good dive preparation is essential to gain the maximum from each day.

Private yacht visitors will find anchorage information, and in addition, the dive site map shows the position of each site. The resident park rangers will be more than happy to assist with any further queries.

It should be pointed out that Cocos Island has a unique history of pirates and buried treasure. It makes pleasant reading during the 30–34 hour crossing or in the quiet evenings on board.

Tuna are among the fastest fish in the world, so quick reflexes and lens are needed to photograph these streamlined beauties.

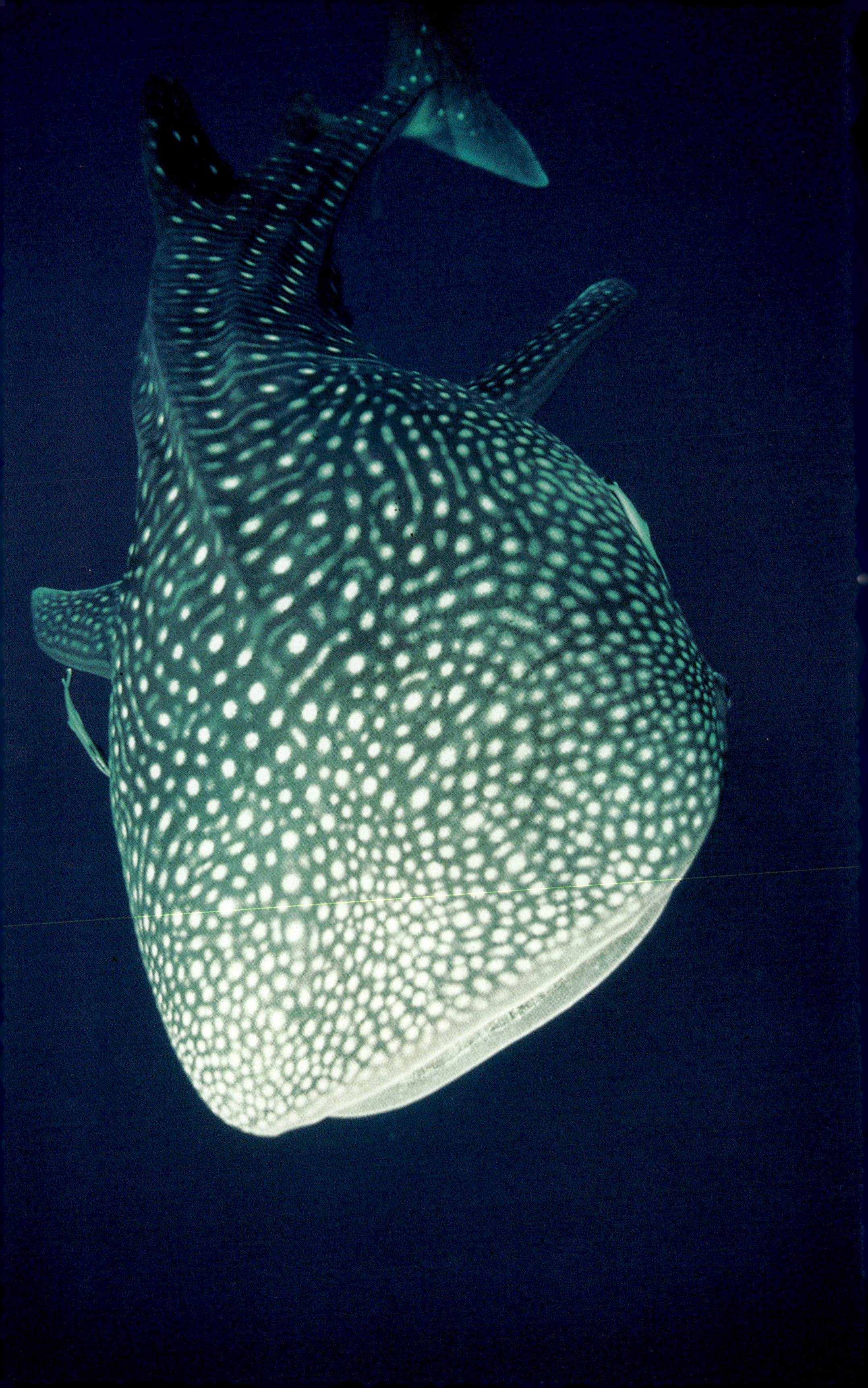

Rating System for Dives and Divers

Divers are rated according to skill. There are three categories: novice, intermediate, and advanced. A **novice** diver is considered to have recently completed a basic diving course or is a certified diver who has not been diving recently or has logged less than 20 dives.

An **intermediate** diver is certified, has been actively diving for at least a year, and has logged more than 20 dives of varying difficulty.

An **advanced** diver has completed an advanced dive course, has experienced drift, night, current, and orienteering diving and has logged more than 100 dives.

Cocos is a single island hundreds of miles from any mainland and offers only open-ocean diving, although most dive sites are adjacent to rocks or small islets. As a safety precaution, throughout the dive, a dinghy follows divers' bubbles and is ready to pick up any diver that surfaces. Cocos is perhaps not the ideal dive destination for novice divers because most dives require intermediate and advanced skill levels. With distractions such as currents, caves, archways, and photography the dive leader will not always be able to assist less experienced divers, while continuing to lead the dive. However, there are a few novice-level dives and a more experienced dive buddy will help. It is a destination that will thrill the adventurer and keen, skilled diver.

Please bear in mind the rating system is only a helpful guide. You must be the judge of your own skills. If you have any reservations about a dive, just sit it out, and wait for the next one. This will be appreciated by your fellow divers and perhaps save an embarrassment.

◄ *A whale shark is one of the most treasured and awesome sights any diver can experience.*

1

Overview of Cocos Island

Cocos Island lies in the east Pacific Ocean, 300 miles off the southwest coast of the Republic of Costa Rica, to which the island belongs. The only means of access to the island is by boat and its natural beauty is immediately apparent on approach.

The first visual impression is of wild, jungle-covered mountains that slope abruptly to the sea, interspersed with bold, perpendicular cliffs. From these cliffs cascade many spectacular waterfalls that almost reach the sea,

The jungle-covered cliffs of Cocos Island are a welcome sight to the weary traveler, whether a 20th century scuba diver or a 16th-century swashbuckler.

giving the impression that someone has left a tap running on top. This is a very welcome sight after the 34-hour boat crossing from Puntarenas.

High above, lush green vegetation covers the vertical rock walls, playing host to a variety of seabirds. Frigate birds, sea eagles, and boobies swoop overhead, diving in and out of the tropical canopy. There is a tangible feeling of mystery about this island.

At first glance, the whole ambience and unique history of the island conjures up images of pirates and buried treasure. It has been suggested that this is the treasure island that Robert Louis Stevenson had in mind when he wrote his famous novel, *Treasure Island.*

This imposing island, only four miles long by two miles wide, remains remote and wild despite various courageous, perhaps futile attempts to harness it. Some of these early efforts at cultivation are still visible on the green slopes of Chatham Bay, but the long arms of the jungle are gaining ground. Clear, blue water laps against the long sandy beach of Wafer Bay. Coconut palms line the crescent-shaped bay and, to the right, a waterfall tumbles down into a pool below.

Here, on Cocos, the fish population has been allowed to grow in harmony with the natural balance of the food chain, which is why such a great diversity and quantity of sea life is prevalent. The area is teeming

Hammerheads are most unusual looking sharks, but their streamlined, elegant, powerful bodies are like any other.

with sharks, rays, massive schools of pelagic and reef fish, turtles, many types of eels, starfish, and even a rare frogfish. The most celebrated resident shark is the scalloped hammerhead. These creatures are here in such numbers, nowadays they are Cocos' most talked about attraction. Richly rewarding encounters with all aforementioned sea life is commonplace, and this has led to Cocos Island becoming one of the most sought-after dive destinations in the world.

Climate

Cocos Island lies in an Intertropical Convergence Zone (I.T.C.Z.). This zone is where the weather patterns of the two hemispheres converge near the equator. Here the north and the southeast trade winds meet with the north and south equatorial currents. The warm north and south equatorial currents run in a westerly direction, which helps create a humid climate. While between the two, the counter equatorial current runs in the opposite direction. Ascending nutrient rich water mixes with these currents as they converge.

Off the coast of Peru, the cold deep waters rise and move northwards forming the Humbolt Current. This current is richly laden with plankton and other food and is this area's major source of food.

These four currents act like giant conveyor-belt food sources, transporting a multitude of nourishment from the different areas from which they originate.

This high rain-forest-clad island, with diverse currents and weather patterns, is rarely seen without some kind of cloud cover and receives 18–24 feet (6–8 meters) of rain annually. The driest season is from January–April, and the wettest season is June–December. Torrential rain and beautiful sunny skies can be expected throughout the year.

Water temperatures are variable, but basically run between 74°–87°F (23°–30°C). Temperatures vary according to depth. Nearer the surface the water is warmer and deeper down it gets colder. Air temperatures range between 68°F–90°F (20°C–33°C).

It is hard to imagine good underwater visibility associated with an area of such high rainfall but, in fact, it has little effect. On one occasion, after

Devil rays are often mistaken for manta rays; however, the backs of devil rays are gray rather than black, their heads are less rounded, and they are generally smaller.

ten hours of torrential rain, which flooded Chatham Bay and turned the water brown, the clouds cleared, the seas calmed, and within two days the underwater visibility was back to normal. At other dive sites farther away from the mainland, these conditions had negligible effects.

Hiking

It is possible to hike to the top of Mount Iglesias, which stands at 634 meters (almost 2,000 ft). Nowadays, it is advisable to be assisted by a guide. Many years ago, a man set off alone and was never seen again. It is thought he fell and broke a leg, became immobile, and without the means to contact help he perished. The climb is fairly hard, through thick vegetation of creeping vines, moss and hanging plants. Once the top is reached, the views are spectacular, and there is a book in which to sign

Hiking through the towering rain forest is hard going, but park rangers are usually available to break the trail and lead enthusiasts up to Mount Iglesias.

The waterfall up-river from Wafer Bay is a most idyllic setting with a wonderful pool. ▶

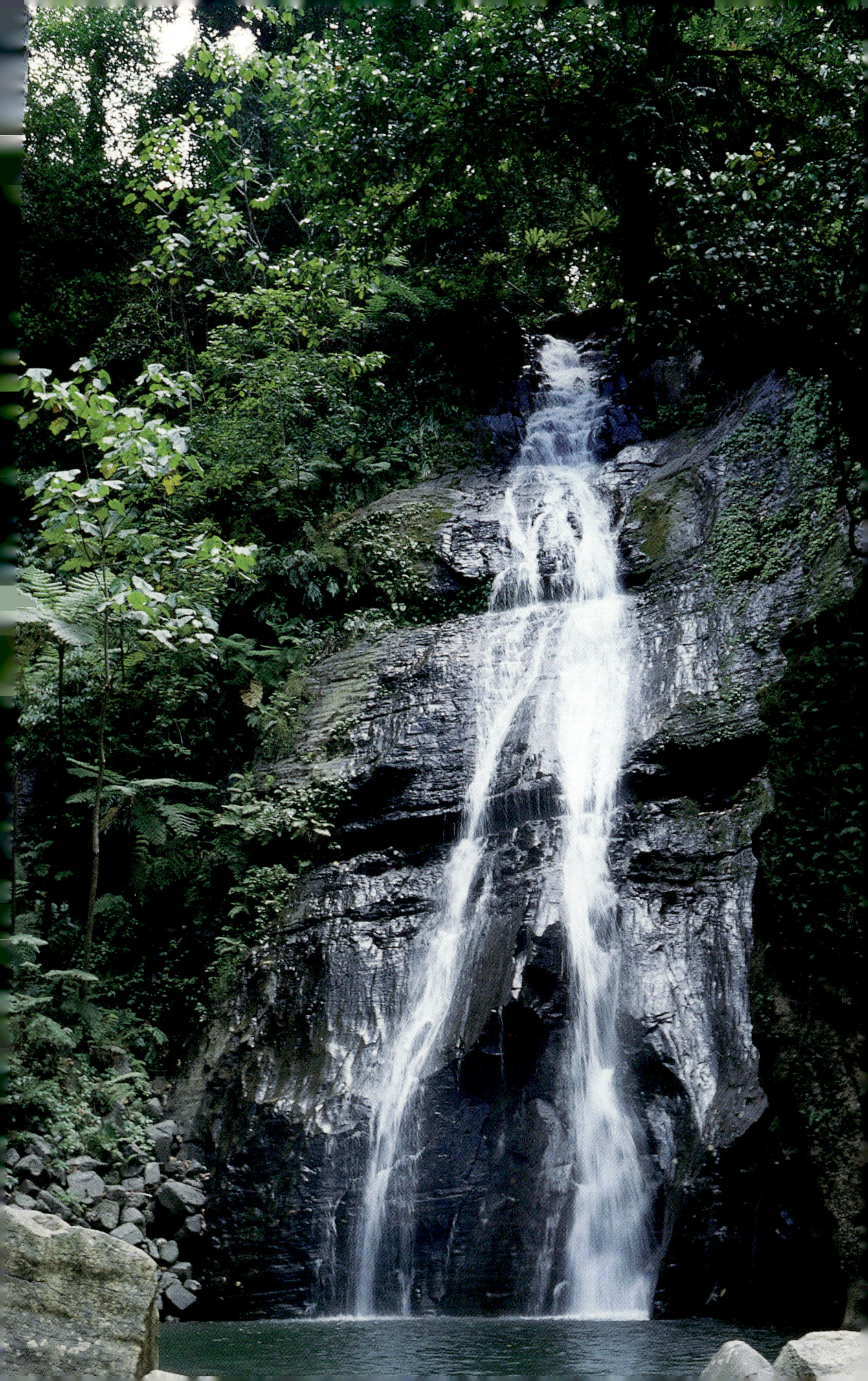

your name and where you are from. There are two much easier and less time-consuming walks. One is up the stream bed at Chatham Bay. The bed is littered with rocks of varying sizes with inscriptions carved by past visitors. Even Cousteau's men left their mark and many others before and after. Some from past centuries make interesting reading and rubbings.

The other walk is up by the side of the river that leads down to Wafer Bay. The going is a bit harder and there are many large holes, left by treasure hunters along the way. The sound of the waterfall can be heard before it is visible. Once seen, it would surely calm a beating heart and loosen the dive tensions of the day. It is a spectacular waterfall plunging some twenty-five feet into an aquamarine pool, ideal for swimming and relaxing.

Geography

Cocos Island arose volcanically, like the Galapagos Islands, during the Pliocene period. This brings it into existence approximately 0.5–1 million years ago. The island, which measures 18 mi^2 (46.6 km^2), was never connected to the mainland. Its flora and fauna did not develop to the same

Live-aboards or private yachts, such as the M/V Ocean Trilogy *pictured here in Weston Bay, are the only way to enjoy Cocos Island.*

extent as the Galapagos', which may have been due to the island's size and weather patterns. A few species of birds, lizards, and freshwater fish are endemic to the island. The Cocos island finch is also known as Darwin's 14th finch.

In 1838, Captain Edward Belcher mapped Cocos island and collected scientific information and specimens, including a finch, which upon return to England, he took to John Gould, who knew Darwin. Darwin was already studying information from his recent expedition to the Galapagos Islands and together they classified the Cocos finch as the 14th finch.

Accommodations

There are **no** hotels or buildings on the island. A small construction in Wafer Bay houses the national park rangers and scientists from Costa Rica. *The only way to visit is by boat.*

There are several fully equipped, modern live-aboard dive boats to choose from, which operate throughout the year. They all offer excellent air-conditioned accommodations, a high level of service, and superb diving facilities. Some even have E6 processing and PAL/NTSC video playback.

Naturally, private yachts are always welcome, but for those who wish to charter one, be advised they may not offer the same facilities as the dive boats.

Cocos Marine Park

Costa Rica designated Cocos Island a marine reserve, or "Area de Conservacion" in 1992. They did this to protect the island from commercial fishing boats and maintain nature's inherent biodiversity. Costa Rica is revered throughout the world for its passive arms policy. They have a natural inclination towards peace and understanding their country's environment. There is no army and their only defense is a national guard that draws from an automatic conscription. Cocos Island usually has 2–3 guards based on the island at all times along with members of the National Park Service.

Wafer Bay is home to the resident guards and park rangers, where there is a newly constructed ranger station. They grow very little, if any, food on the island and rely heavily on the licensed dive boats for supplies. Occasionally, Costa Rican scientists and students are allowed to visit the island, but are not resident.

There is a 5-mile (9-km) exclusion zone around the island for commercial fishing boats. For the most part they seem to keep their distance, despite the park rangers having only a small, poorly powered motor boat at their disposal.

Visiting yachts can stay anchored for up to a month. But first they must check-in with the ranger station and pay a park fee.

View of dive sites Dos Amigos I and II from the summit of Mount Iglesias.

History and Treasure

For those wishing to visit the island with a view to treasure hunting, it is too late. The government will not issue any more licenses for treasure hunting in the foreseeable future.

Widely believed to have been discovered between 1514 and 1542, this tiny island was first named Santa Cruz. Discovered by an off-course Spanish ship, it was named after the feast day of the holy cross on which it was found. The new world colonies of Spain, between Baja California and Guayaquil, had been producing incredible wealth and sending it back regularly to their mother country. These richly laden Spanish galleons were frequently intercepted and looted by many buccaneers through the 16th, 17th, and 18th centuries.

Many boulders bearing the names, dates, and even messages of past visitors, some more than 100 years old, are found along the river bed that runs into Chatham Bay.

Cocos Island was a small uninhabited island many weeks sailing from the nearest mainland. Here travelers could find food, fuel, water, and shelter, so it became renowned as an ideal safe haven. Over a period of centuries many notorious buccaneers such as Edward Davis, Benito Bonito, and William Thompson sailed their heavily laden ships to unload their booty, rest, re-supply, and plan their next conquest. Many pirates drew maps to relocate their buried hoard at a later date. Some maps have been found, but, to this date, it is believed that very little treasure has ever been recovered.

During the 16th century, Sir Francis Drake would undoubtedly have been among the early visitors. Described as a gentlemen pirate, Drake plundered Spanish towns and sacked their ships. He did so by command of the Queen of England who, at this time, was at war with Spain. In 1577, he sailed with the *Golden Hind* for the South Seas.

His most spectacular prize was the Spanish ship, *Cacafuego,* from which he took 13 chests of silver coins, 80 lbs of gold and numerous boxes of jewels. He arrived in Portsmouth in September 1580, the second man to sail round the world.

The late 17th century brought visiting adventurers and pirates. It was these men who renamed the island Cocos or Isle del Cocos because of the abundance of coconut palms that grew there. One ship's log mentions taking on board 2,000 coconuts for the ongoing voyage. Today, coconut trees form only a small part of the abundant flora and fauna.

The anchorage of many pirate ships over the centuries, Chatham Bay is still the best anchorage (harbor) on Cocos Island.

One notable pirate was Captain Edward Davis. He started his swashbuckling career aboard *Bachelor's Delight* in 1684, and spent 20 years plundering Spanish ships and cities up and down the coast of South America.

Captain Davis and his men made Cocos Island their base. They probably landed in Chatham Bay where they divided the treasure and buried it on the island. After refitting the ships, loading fresh provisions, and resting his men, Davis set out for further adventure.

Among his companions were two Englishmen, William Dampier and Dr. Lionel Wafer. Dampier went on to make a name for himself as an adventurer and writer. His journals were popular in his time and are still today, but now are increasingly hard to come by. The southernmost point of the island bears his name. Lionel Wafer was a naturalist and a surgeon. Although he traveled with pirates, he took no part in the raids. He had an exploring nature and spent many years studying the cultures of South America. He wrote extensively of his experiences.

Between 1788–1840, European whalers used Cocos Island as a stop-off for water and supplies. There were no fishing restrictions at this time.

Consequently, they depleted the whale population to such an extent that the price plummeted and the industry collapsed.

In 1794, Captain George Vancouver visited Cocos and spent many weeks there. He describes it as being a "valuable little island." In commemoration of his visit he directed his men to cut in a rock the date of their arrival, the commanders, and the vessels. This joined marks inscribed by past visitors, some of which are still visible on the rocks leading up the river in Chatham Bay.

Chatham Bay is named after a ship. The *Chatham* was a 131-ton armed brig, built by the British Admiralty as a survey vessel. It has been noted as visiting Cocos Island in 1794 at least once.

In 1818, Captain Bennet Graham, a British naval officer, was sent to survey the coast between Panama and Cape Horn. Captain Graham soon adopted a career of piracy. With his ship H.M.S. *Devonshire* he captured many Spanish galleons and sailed for Cocos to bury the treasure. He soon realized the British authorities were on to him but could not avoid being captured and later executed. Just before his capture he handed his treasure map to a crew member. Although the crew member returned to Cocos Island, his recovery efforts were unsuccessful. The "Devonshire Treasure" is said to comprise 350 tons of bullion, and reportedly still lies in its resting place on the island.

Around this time there was another blood thirsty pirate named Benito Bonito. He was the terror of the Atlantic until 1819, when the British Admiralty sent two ships after him. Bonito, at this point, decided to try his luck on the west coast of America. He rounded Cape Horn and set about looting every ship he encountered, plundering towns and robbing church treasures on his way up to Mexico. Among other prizes was a Spanish ship laden with gold destined to pay the armies in Spain.

At Acapulco, he learned that gold was brought down from the mountains and turned over to armed guards near the city. By masquerading as local guards, they took over the next consignment and loaded it onto their ship, without having to fire a single shot. They now found themselves with unimaginable wealth, and at the same time realized they were susceptible to attack from other pirates. Bonito, therefore, went to Cocos Island, where he announced plans to make it his headquarters. However, his men had other ideas; they wanted to leave the island with their share of the treasures. After violent and bloody words the crew agreed to bury it on the island.

Bonito couldn't handle his share without help. He directed a dozen men to haul his chests on land and led them blindfolded to a secret spot, where they buried his hoard. With his two aides, Thompson and Chapelle, Bonito took coordinates and drew a map, with the intention of returning at some later time. This never occurred.

Bonito double-crossed Thompson and Chapelle, which led them to be captured by the British authorities. In return for immunity, they led the British to Bonito's hideout in the West Indies, where he was caught and killed. Thompson and Chapelle were set free, but didn't make it back to Cocos either. Both men died poor.

Stories of buccaneers and pirates depositing great quantities of treasure on Cocos Island are varying in their authenticity. As almost none of the said hoards have ever been recovered, it is not possible to determine how accurate they are. However, it is accepted that there is no other island in the region like Cocos Island, and judging from old maps and new, it has structurally changed to a great degree over the past centuries. For instance, there was once a large, inland, freshwater lake, which visitors used for bathing. Due, presumably, to some form of ground movement it no longer exists. All around the island, cliffs have tumbled away, covering once accessible caves and grottoes.

Over the past century, treasure hunters have left their mark. The area around Wafer Bay has been picked, scraped, shoveled, and blasted out of all likeness to its former appearance. One such treasure hunter was Augustus Gissler. He was so determined to succeed, where others had failed, he and his wife lived on Cocos for more than twenty years. In 1888, the island was claimed by Costa Rica, and nine years later they nominated him as governor. Gissler made several attempts to colonize the island, but the hard, lonely life was too much for the settlers. His spirit broken from long years of disappointment, Gissler finally gave up. He departed Cocos in 1908, never having found the illusive treasures.

From the early 1900s to present day, there have been many costly, courageous attempts to find treasure. They even include a past U.S. president, an English nobleman, and several unauthorized naval officers. Nowadays treasure hunting is outlawed, as it is throughout much of the world.

The Great Treasure of Lima*. There is more than one version of this story, but they all agree over its principal features—the amount of the treasure, its hiding-place, and the identity of the chief villain.

The viceroy of Peru, holding court from Lima, had jurisdiction from the Andes to Patagonia. It was his responsibility to convey to Spain the royal share of the taxes and precious metals and jewels mined throughout the territories. With the sea routes to Spain endangered, he was unable to send the annual dues for some years, and so the wealth accumulated.

By 1822, Simon Bolivar, the great liberator of South America, had already freed Venezuela, New Grenada, and Quito from Spanish authority. He then set his sights on Peru. In Lima, the viceroy and the ecclesiastic officials heard of the advancing troops. Rather than risk capture and lose the hoards of

---

*While this story is well documented, some details have been taken from the book *Cocos Island—Old Pirates' Haven* by Christopher Weston, Imprenta y Litografia, Trejos, 1990.

If the waters around Cocos don't provide enough adventure, a walk through the jungle along the river bed near Wafer Bay will add some terrestrial excitement. ▶

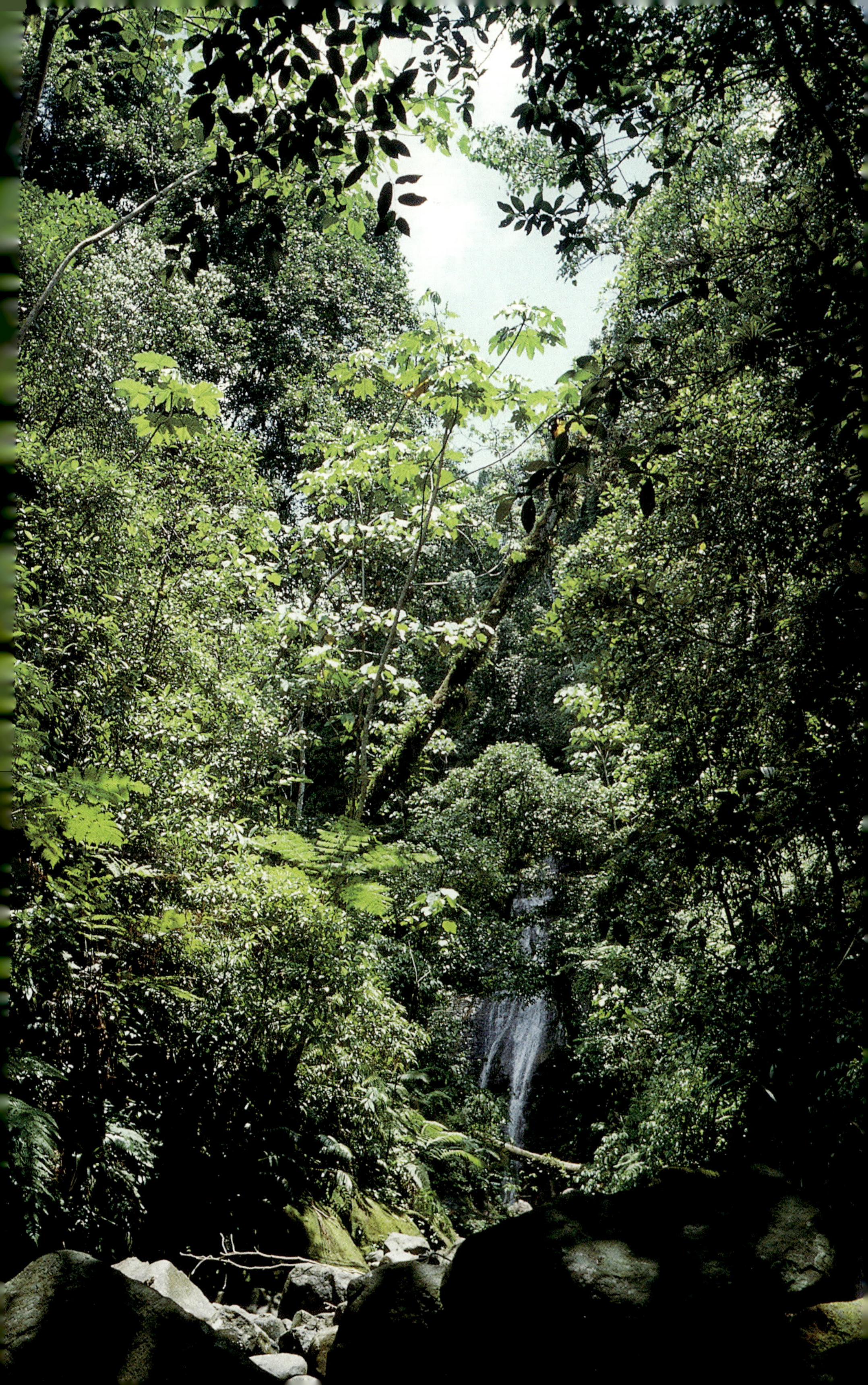

Buried pirate's treasure may be the lure for Cocos "landlubbers," but the real treasures are found in the island's natural beauty above and below the water, such as this jeweled boxfish.

riches, they decided to ship their combined wealth out of the country. Once the treasure had safely been moved to the port of Callao, they set about finding a suitable ship. Unfortunately, there were no Spanish galleons or warships in the port. Instead, the British merchant ship *Mary Dear,* was at anchor, commanded by Captain William Thompson. At that time, he had been trading along the Peruvian coast for some years and was known and trusted by them. So, the treasure was transferred to *Mary Dear.* The plan was that the laden *Mary Dear* would cruise around for a few months until word was received to return or deliver the treasure to the Spanish in Panama.

One night in August 1821, the *Mary Dear* put to sea with a hold full of priceless treasures. The most valuable item, apart from the gold and silver bullion, was a solid gold, life-size image of the Virgin Mary, encrusted with jewels. The size and value of the treasure was too tempting for captain and crew. Before morning, the guards and priests had been killed and dumped overboard. Now the problem of hiding the treasure rested on Thompson's shoulders.

The coast and ports were patrolled by troops and ships, which made it impossible to pick-up supplies for a long voyage. Captain Thompson suggested they sail for Cocos Island, where they could stash the treasure without fear of capture and return at a later date to recover it. The men readily agreed and after a few weeks at sea the *Mary Dear* sailed into one of the picturesque bays, dropped anchor, and proceeded to relinquish her valuable cargo. Many trips were made before all the booty was transferred ashore, where it was buried in one spot. Only a few coins were shared out among the crew. That was the last anyone saw of the great treasure of Lima.

The Exotic Lure of Cocos Island. Nowadays, with widespread travel reaching all corners of the earth, few places remain unaffected by tourism. With the only access by sea, it is unlikely that mass tourism will ever have a chance to take hold on Cocos Island. There are no airports or hotels. It is because of this that the island has been able to keep its natural beauty and mysterious charm. It lacks luxury, but offers a unique opportunity to absorb the atmosphere and revel in the freedom of an uninhabited island. For divers and non-divers alike there is an abundance of beautiful scenery and wildlife to capture on film. A variety of wildflowers, plants, and birds offer great photographic opportunities. Escape the home crowds, spend a day on the beach alone with only the noise of seabirds and lapping waves to keep you company.

This cyclone of swirling jacks provides a rare spectacle of orderly chaos.

2

Diving in Cocos Island

This truly is an island of treasures. Aside from the buried variety, there is another, more accessible treasure beneath the surrounding deep blue sea. Below the rolling waves, there exists an enchanted world begging to be explored. Dramatic underwater seascapes provide the perfect scenery for a profusion of aquatic performers. Powerful displays of sharks, rays, and other spectacular marine life make this one of the most spellbinding, vibrant, underwater theaters in the world.

The most notable performers are the huge numbers of scalloped hammerhead sharks. Unlike other parts of the world, where hammerhead sharks are known to congregate at certain times of the year, there seems to be no particular seasonal attraction to this island; they are present throughout the year. Encounters with shoals of up to 200 or more of these majestic sharks are found at a variety of the island's dive sites. Dirty Rock has the largest concentration and Cousteau's Sea Mount, which is rarely dived, plays host to great families of these bizarre, magnificent, and fearsome marine creatures.

While the hammerhead sharks are a considerable attraction in themselves, many other fascinating spectacles await divers. In the beautiful, blue, clear water that surrounds the island, observers can watch oceanic, silky, whitetip reef sharks and whale sharks. Coming face to face with a marble ray is almost a certainty, as there are so many of them. Plus there are manta rays, eagle rays, and devil rays, which have been known to glide among divers decompressing at the end of a dive.

Nearly all dive sites can boast enormous schools of pelagic fish, most notably from the family of jacks. Barracuda and tuna are also present along with sightings of marlin and sailfish. The reefs are teeming with snapper, grunts, goatfish, palmetos, rainbow runners, and triggerfish to name a few. Dolphins are not uncommon visitors to the island, but underwater encounters are rare.

While sighting a whale shark is not a regular occurrence, many scuba divers have had chance meetings here. Classified as the biggest fish in the sea, this beguiling character can grow to a massive 50 ft (16 m). While its prodigious size is both alarming and intimidating, it is in fact a harmless plankton eater, and so poses no threat to a scuba diver. The sheer size and presence of a whale shark are usually enough to deter eager divers or

Cocos Island

Map labels:
- Manuelita Island (6, 7)
- Punta Agiyas
- Weston Bay
- Chatham Bay (11)
- Dirty Rock (1)
- Wafer Bay (12)
- National Park Ranger Station
- Punta Gissler
- Punta Maria
- Marble Ray Point (10)
- Mount Iglesias 2,079 ft. (634 m)
- Monteone Island
- Rodrigues Bay
- Calypso Falls
- Cousteau's Sea Mount
- Dos Amigos I (4)
- Dos Amigos II (5)
- Juan Bautista Island
- Iglesias Bay
- Submerged Rock (2)
- (8)
- Sharkfin Rock (3)
- Dampier Head
- Manta Ray Point (9)

assailants from close contact. Diving within close proximity to such an enormous shark, without risk of personal injury is, for most people, a big enough thrill. Unhappy experiences can result from contact and worse still could cause the shark to retreat.

This prolific marine life is set in breathtaking underwater seascapes where time and the course of nature have carved tunnels, points, pinnacles, and great archways in the island's rock. Many of these tunnels and archways contain myriad fish, lobsters, starfish, and eels. They form a natural safe haven from the tiresome currents and hungry predators.

Diving is predominantly deep, below 100 feet (30 m), and extensive decompression stops are required after lengthy dives. As divers know, pro-

Dolphins have been spotted and heard around Cocos, but they are rarely seen during dives.

longed pressure at depth causes nitrogen bubbles to pass into the blood via the lungs. Nitrogen bubbles expand when outside pressure decreases. So a slow, steady ascent is necessary to allow as much nitrogen as possible to leave the blood. Decompression stops, between 10–20 feet (3–7 m), act as the final precautionary stage. They allow most of the remaining nitrogen to pass out of the blood before surfacing. These stages could be anything between 5 and 30 minutes. If these stops are not obeyed, residual nitrogen could expand on surfacing, causing pain, otherwise known as "the bends."

Sometimes at dusk the large pinky-red sun illuminates the night sky and glistens, like sparkling crystal, on the flickering sea. The peace and natural beauty of the island is enchanting and will leave you with unforgettable memories of the experience.

With twelve dive sites to choose from and a wide range of fast-changing weather conditions to contend with, you should remain flexible when planning dives, whether you are on a dive boat or your own yacht. Some dive sites are only safe in very calm seas and, therefore, planning a week's diving can be very difficult. The daily routine should be planned each morning or, at the earliest, the night before. Some dive boat captains will make the choice for you—an ideal solution, because they have local experience of swell and storms that can build up quickly.

It's easy to see how Cocos Island may have been the treasure island Robert Louis Stevenson had in mind when he wrote his famous novel.

The are many diving spots around this island that are not included in this list. The dives mentioned here are the most popular and most often visited. There could be others the live-aboard captains have discovered themselves.

Dirty Rock   1

Currents:	Varying from nothing to very strong, depending on the time of day
Visibility:	Best, 100+ ft (30+ m), first thing in the morning, to not less than 70 ft (25 m)
Surge:	More often than not, but not horrendous
Anchorage:	Not possible
Sea state:	An unprotected rock, so usually choppy; sometimes pounding waves

Also known as Pietra Socia and Boat Rock, Dirty Rock lies in the calmer northern region, off Punta Gissler, just a short dinghy ride from the most popular anchorages. It lies about one-half mile (1,000 m) off the mainland and receives an abundance of nutrient-rich currents, which sustain not only the huge shark and fish populations, but also an extensive range of flourishing healthy corals found on the northeast side.

Every kind of marine species affiliated with the Cocos area seems to be attracted to this rock, including the highest concentration of scalloped hammerhead sharks with which close encounters are virtually guaranteed.

Divers can drop in anywhere around the rock. However, a safe and popular place to start is on the south side. Entering the water near here can mean descending through clouds of blue creole fish; below at 100 ft (30 m), sharks

The jagged features of Dirty Rock host scores of seabirds.

Schooling scalloped hammerhead sharks are present year-round at Dirty Rock and close encounters are virtually guaranteed. (Photo: Sam Harwood)

are already visible. On this side, near to the rock, there is a tall pinnacle and, nestling at the base, is a large school of yellow snappers. Move along with the current in a westerly direction, keeping the wall on the right.

Along the sloping south side between a depth of 80–140 ft (25–45 m) are large boulders, and many whitetip sharks can be seen resting on the sandy areas. This is where the action is! On the first dive of the day this is the most exciting place to be. Hammerhead sharks are here in numbers, along with whitetip reef sharks, tuna fish, bluefin jacks, rainbow runners, marble rays, and reef fish.

Hammerhead sharks can be seen milling around, above and below, going off and regrouping but with no clear pattern. Close encounters are random and totally unprovoked. Never forget that these creatures are indiscriminate, powerful ocean predators that can attack their prey swiftly and silently.

Lower down at 150 ft (45 m) or more the slope levels out to an open sandy bottom. Hammerheads may be found here, where the visibility is not so good and the depth limits bottom time.

Approaching the end of the island, a massive rock formation or mountain appears to the left. This, together with the island, forms a wide canyon. The canyon itself is quite spectacular. It plunges down to 140 ft (42 m) and both sides gradually slope away upwards with niches and jagged pointed edges. Passage through here is almost blocked by a massive

Whale sharks visit Cocos from time to time and are usually found in the shallower waters around Dirty Rock.

school of silver snappers. Marble rays and sharks cruise through, breaking up for an instant their otherwise perfect formation. A mid-morning dive can sometimes capture the sun shining down directly behind them. It is roughly in this area that whale sharks have been spotted.

The aforementioned mountain must not be ignored. From a depth of 200 ft (60 m) or more, it rises up to within 30 ft (10 m) of the surface. The walls are barren and slope quite steeply. If the hammerhead sharks have not been found along the south wall, then they may be found at greater depths off the far side of this mound.

Towards the end of a dive, the current will usually take a diver to the north side. A decompression stop is almost always necessary. During stop times, visits by manta rays are a possibility. These majestic creatures, which resemble underwater birds, glide, twist, and swirl around. They are known throughout the world for their inquisitiveness and fearless approaches. They can hover motionless in a strong current or move with exceptional speed. The power and agility their wings provide is awesome.

Submerged Rock   2

Currents:	Stronger farther out and little in some places on the rock
Visibility:	Between 60–100 ft (18–30 m), no run-off problems
Surge:	Strong nearly all the time above 50 ft (15 m)
Anchorage:	None
Sea state:	Usually choppy and prone to swells

Located about a mile (1,500 m) southeast from the mouth of Iglesias Bay, in the southern region of the island, Submerged Rock is an uncharted hazard that just breaks the surface. The latest corrections to the admiralty chart in 1988 did not include this rock, but a revision is currently underway.

Underwater, this rock plunges down both sharply and gradually. It is broken up with large ledges, some with sandy bottoms, and an outer pinnacle. The colorful, prolific fish life gives relief to the harsh contours of the reef. Sometimes the fish gather in such numbers that they momentarily blot out the sun.

Whitetip reef sharks are present in quantity and some of the females have mating scars, inflicted by over-excited males during coupling. Encounters with bigeye jacks, tuna, and silky sharks can be expected.

This tunnel at Submerged Rock is full of blue-striped snapper and an occasional whitetip shark.

Submerged Rock hosts many reef whitetip sharks; some females bear mating scars.

Near the surface thousands of Creole fish mass and momentarily blot out the sun.

Hammerhead sharks are reputed to school farther out, where the current is very strong, and extreme caution is recommended. *Remember, you are hundreds of miles from medical help.*

In the northern section, at 80 ft (25 m), there is a flat patch that lies at the entrance to a small busy tunnel. Approximately 20 ft (6 m) high and 9 ft (3 m) wide, this tunnel is so crammed with fish that it is quite easy to miss it altogether. The fish that congregate here—blue-striped snapper, squirrelfish, yellow goatfish—do so to escape the current and sharks. This is easily the liveliest section of the rock and, fortunately, is in shallow water. Swimming in and out of the tunnel can be quite tricky. In the shallow waters around the rock, a heavy surge pushes and pulls floating objects, rendering any powers of direction virtually useless.

This dive is also known for the many cleaning stations and octopus. An excellent dive site when more interesting sites are inaccessible due to bad weather.

Sharkfin Rock 3

Currents: Variable, up to 1 knot in some places
Visibility: Very good, 90+ ft (27+ m)
Surge: Shallow areas only
Anchorage: None
Sea state: Unprotected, usually choppy

Located to the southwest, off Dampier Head, as the name suggests, this rock resembles a shark's fin. Only 6 ft (2 m) high, this rock plunges down to great depths, and is best known for a huge school of bigeye jacks.

During a dive, it is quite possible to go around the entire rock. The island side harbors whitetip sharks and marble rays, at times, lying on the sand. The jack school tends to congregate on the outer side, where there is often some current.

The school can vary from 50 up to several thousand. They make a very impressive image when they pass by like a never-ending silver stream or form a massive swirling spiral. Jacks do have an amazing capacity to move together in the most fabulous ways, and when light touches their shiny, silver skin, their graceful movements are greatly enhanced.

There are very few places in the world where jacks can be seen in these huge numbers, and certainly pose a difficult but spectacular photographic subject.

The namesake of this dive site breaks the surface with just 6 feet (2 m) of rock, making it truly look like a prowling shark.

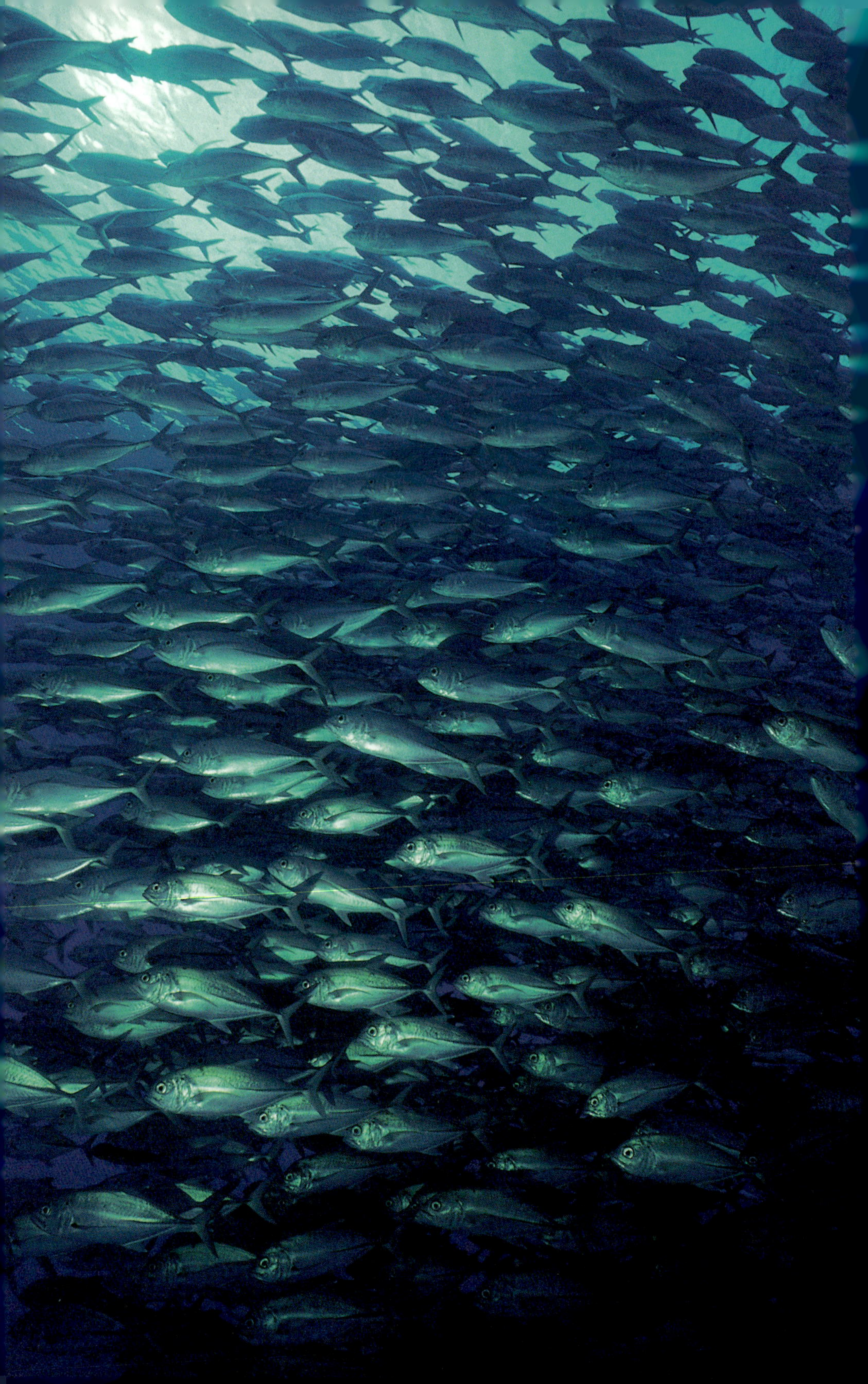

Dos Amigos I 4

Current: Very strong on one side
Visibility: Excellent, 100+ ft (30+ m)
Surge: Little, only near surface
Anchorage: None
Sea state: Unprotected, so choppy

Cocos offers many thrilling dives but this is the most spectacular underwater vista. This island juts up out of the sea with sheer cliffs all the way round, totally inaccessible except to the resident birds. Underwater, the cliff walls continue down to varying depths, broken up by ledges and niches, where marine life congregates. Because of strong currents on the north side of this island, dives start on the south side. It is advisable to drop in anywhere along this side and continue round, keeping the wall on your left.

As you near the end of the wall, an enormous deep archway will appear. The sun pours through from above, and schooling fish, suspended in the entrance, are shrouded in light. Inside this subaquatic cathedral the walls seem to come alive, merge with one another, and then part, leaving a trail

◄ *A silver stream of schooling bigeye jacks passes by at Sharkfin Rock.*

A diver surrounded by snappers explores the great archway at Dos Amigos I.

Many blue-striped snappers congregate along the reef wall.

of sparkling light in all directions. Light dances off every surface and the mass of fish and sharks tease and tantalize the eye and the camera lens. It is important not to use up too much bottom time before you arrive at the archway, because the bottom is at 95 ft (29 m) and you will want to stay as long as possible. The snapper school congregating in the archway must be 300 strong. They pose a challenging subject to capture on film.

Dos Amigos II   5

Current: Farther out, medium strong
Visibility: Excellent, 100+ ft (30+ m)
Surge: None
Anchorage: None
Sea state: Unprotected, therefore choppy

This, the outer of the two islands, is similar in appearance above water to its brother, but not below. It descends much deeper into the depths and, diving at 100 ft (30 m) with 90-ft (27-m) visibility, it is not possible to see the bottom.

The dive site is halfway along, on the north side, of an otherwise featureless sloping wall. At about 140 ft (43 m) a series of massive boulders rests on sand and rock and harbors schools of snappers and many types of rays. Here, some large snappers are so huge that they make the whitetip sharks look insignificant.

Red snappers dance in the dive light at Dos Amigos II.

A large marble ray plays host to a juvenile pilot fish.

Large, curious hammerhead sharks and small schools of rays cruise past this outer area, using the ever-present current as a food conveyor belt. This is an exciting deep dive and on a sunny day will provide fabulous entertainment.

Manuelita Island West   6

Current: Very strong, but not always present
Visibility: Excellent, 90+ ft (27+ m)
Surge: Strong around and near rock, even below 50 ft (15 m)
Sea state: Sometimes quite calm

Manuelita Island is situated off Punta Agiyas, which juts out between the famous Chatham Bay and Weston Bay, and offers two of Cocos' best dive sites. This little island lies north to south and strong currents are found on both sides at various times of the day.

The west side is a deep drift dive with a wall profile, broken up with large boulders that fall away to a sandy bottom at 140 ft (43 m). Lurking among these boulders are moray eels, lobsters, turtles, and a variety of vividly colored fish, such as blue-striped snappers, trumpetfish, squirrelfish, and hawkfish. Whitetip and hammerhead sharks circle around

Marble rays are so numerous and active at this dive site that contact with divers only seems to be avoidable because of the ray's agility.

35

above and below, keeping a watchful eye on their visitors. Between the boulders, it is possible to escape the current, and divers with a camera have the time to set up some good shots.

Farther out, along the large sandy area, schooling hammerheads can be found. However, the visibility is much worse and the opportunity for quality photography is limited.

Along this side you may encounter a never-ending stream of silvery jacks. These fish are pelagic, which means their habitat is in the deeper regions between 120–600 ft (36–180 m). While the school of jacks average 300 strong, they tend to move around in smaller groups of 30 or so, which sometimes include a whitetip shark. Jacks and other fish have been known to brush themselves along the backs of sharks, using the shark's rough skin in an effort to remove parasites from themselves.

Slightly beyond the boulders, divers are carried by the current to a more vertical wall with very little growth, other than collections of small organisms such as sponges, tunicates, corals, and algae. It is worth trying to slip away from the current's clutches at some point along the wall because,

Be alert divers! Don't forget to look behind because there may be an inquisitive hammerhead on your tail.

Vivid rainbow jacks pass by in the current at Manuelita West.

among this colorful intricate, miniature world, lies the smallest of fish, the blenny. This tiny fish leads a hermit-like existence, taking over vacated homes such as barnacles. Full of character, they lie in these small, purloined grottoes with their heads poking out, watching the world go by. Because they are by no means strong swimmers, they dart in and out, catching morsels of food as the current carries them past.

Manuelita Island East   7

Currents: Not usually found on the reef, only farther out over the sand
Visibility: 60–100 ft (18–30 m), this area is affected by run-off
Surge: None on the reef area
Anchorage: Possible but not recommended, because of damage to coral
Sea state: Usually calm

The east side is quite different. The crescent shoreline forms a protected shallow bay, which is ideally suited to afternoon and night dives and snorkeling. Coral heads start at a depth of 25 ft (8 m) and gradually slope down to a flat sandy bottom at 40 ft (12 m). This reef abounds with juvenile marine creatures, a natural aquatic nursery tucked away from the ripping current. This side offers a tremendous variety of fish: jacks, rainbow runners, milkfish, grunts, goatfish, snappers, parrotfish, butterflyfish, puffer-

An orange frogfish perches on a rock at Manuelita East.

Yellow goatfish pass over the reef at Manuelita East.

fish, boxfish, and turtles to name a few. One of the highlights of this dive are frogfish. Their color and size vary enormously. This, coupled with the fact that they rest motionless on the reef, make them extremely difficult to distinguish. The largest frogfish found here is 1 ft (30 cm) long, and is bright orange.

Farther out, where the reef meets the sand, the diversity of life intensifies. Numerous whitetip sharks lie on the bottom allowing for a good photo opportunity. Hammerhead sharks and turtles coast past and pelagic fish come here to spawn and visit "cleaning stations."

The sandy seabed plays host to an assortment of creatures. Ocean triggerfish make shallow nests in the sand. Tiny bluespotted blennies hover at the entrance to their neat holes and dart down into them whenever predators approach, and schools of yellow goatfish forage around in the sand, feeding on the tiny micro-organisms they disturb.

At night, the roles reverse, and those that lurked inside the reef during the day come out to feed; an assortment of eels, squirrelfish, starfish, brit-

Only seen at night, this shy zebra eel peeks out from a reef hideaway.

The Manuelita East reef area is often visited by turtles.

Large pelagic are exciting to see, but even tiny creatures, such as this hermit crab, offer remarkable sights.

tle stars, and yellow cup coral to name a few. Whitetip sharks are also present at night. At times they can be overly inquisitive, suddenly appearing in dive lights and even bumping into divers, but not in an aggressive way.

This is a highly recommended day or night dive where you can take a break from the deep drift dives and calmly study the reef life more closely.

There is a story about a diver who had a rather unusual experience with a friendly turtle, where for fifteen minutes she played with it, rubbing its tummy and the underside of its neck. The turtle seemed to enjoy every minute of the fuss and the encounter came to an end only because the diver ran out of air.

Cousteau's Sea Mount   8

Currents:	Very strong, ½–2 knots
Visibility:	Good, 90 ft (27 m)
Surge:	None
Anchorage:	Only for small boats waiting for divers, not overnight
Sea state:	Unprotected, usually choppy

This mount lies approximately 1 mile (1.6 km) off the southeast coast, between Monteone Island and Juan Bautista Island. This dive site is also known as Alcyone, and if the licensed dive boats can't find it, then it is not really a viable proposition. But once found, drop over a weighted marker buoy, where anchorage is not feasible for large yachts, then immediately send down the divers. Alternatively, if the sea is calm, anchor a tender boat and put down a shot line, which the divers can follow down.

At a depth of 150 ft (46 m), this roundish mound of barren rock looms up from the sandy bottom, creating an eerie feeling. The highest point is at a depth of 80 ft (25 m). There are no striking features and few colorful fish to catch the eye, just a few sandy lee spots that many resting whitetips share with moray eels.

Many reef whitetip sharks can be found resting in sandy niches around this sea mount.

Encountering a 10-ft (3-m) silvertip shark in open water will get the adrenalin flowing and the heart pounding.

Part of the thrill of diving this sea mount is that Jacque Cousteau found it while on an exploratory visit here. The main attraction of this site is schooling hammerheads. The school encountered here had many juveniles in tow, and these adorable, miniature creatures of varying sizes had to swim fast to keep up with their more graceful parents. They were not so easy to approach and moved away at the slightest movement.

There is a strong prevailing current running to the northeast, which affects descent and ascent. To be on the safe side, ascending divers should inflate an attached buoy, especially during any decompression. This should ensure they are picked up quickly before adverse conditions occur.

Manta Ray Point 9

Current:	Medium strength, but not all the time
Visibility:	In good weather conditions 80+ ft (25 m)
Surge:	None
Anchorage:	None
Sea state:	A very exposed area, usually bad

Cabo Dampier, meaning Dampier Head, is located on the southwest side of Cocos Island. There is a rock off this point where the constant choppy sea sends up clouds of spray on impact. Here, beneath the surge and churning sea, is a dive that offers a chance of manta ray encounters.

It may be necessary to dive below 90 ft (27 m) to find these curious creatures but, once found, they have been known to accompany divers for

Devil rays, which are often mistaken for mantas, are also frequent visitors to this area. ▶

The peaceful and seemingly effortless "flight" of manta rays is a common spectacle around Manta Ray Point.

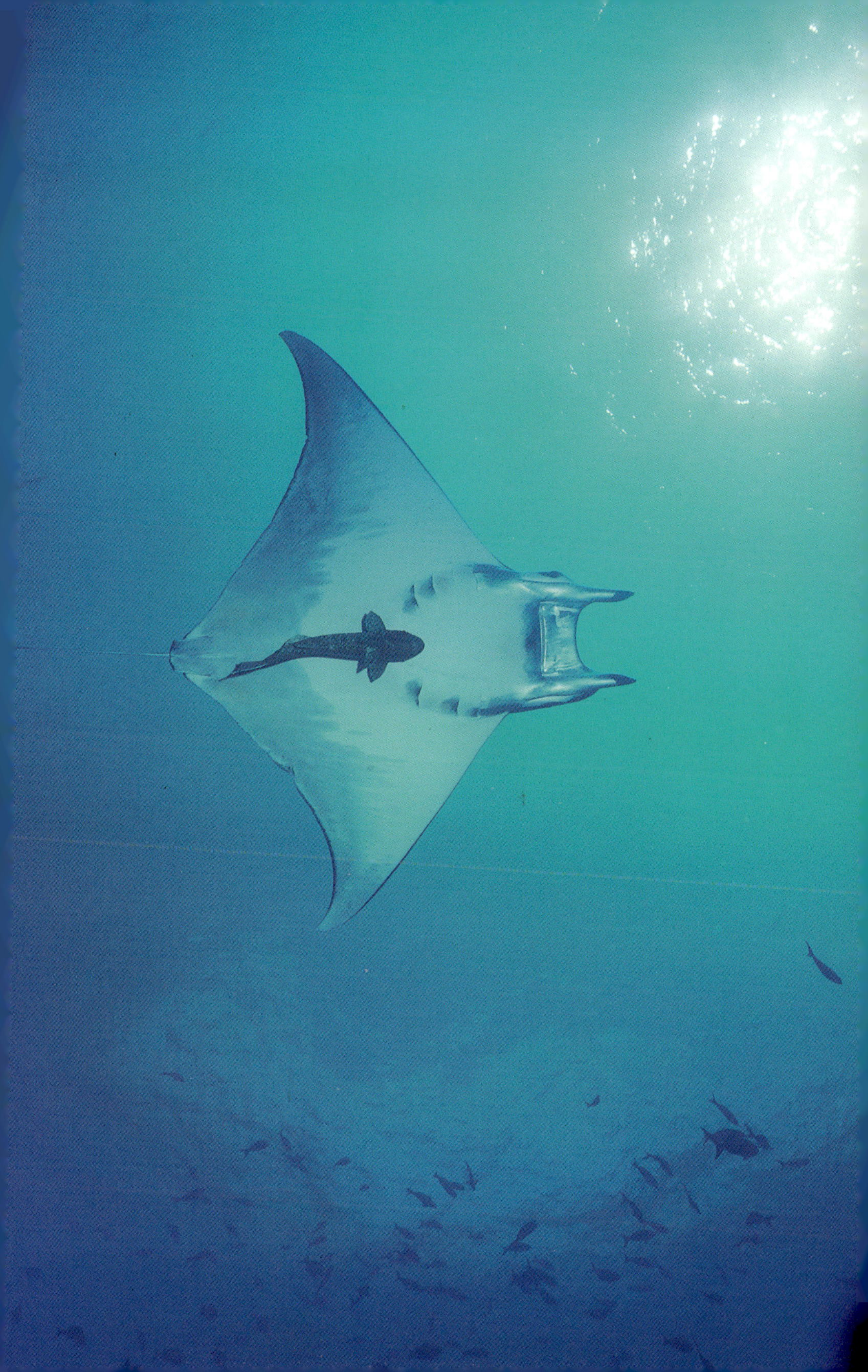

Manta Ray Point attracts many pelagics such as these rainbow runners.

A trumpetfish uses a sea fan as camouflage. ▶

the duration of the dive. There is no reef growth in the area, therefore it is a "what's passing" dive.

Manta rays are the most elegant member of the ray family and also the most beautiful. They have white bellies and dark gray/black backs, and sometimes have distinguishing marks. They have two cephalic fins on either side of their mouth cavity that they use to guide food in while they feed. It is a remarkable site watching a manta ray feed. With mouths wide open they swirl through a cloud of plankton performing a "loop the loop" over and over again.

They are quite friendly towards divers, but be warned they don't like the bubbles exhaled from regulators. Mantas have a certain resemblance to birds. With undulating wing movements and silent motion soaring, the likeness is striking. Manta rays are perfectly streamlined, allowing efficient movement through the water. A simple flick of a wing and they are impossible to keep up with.

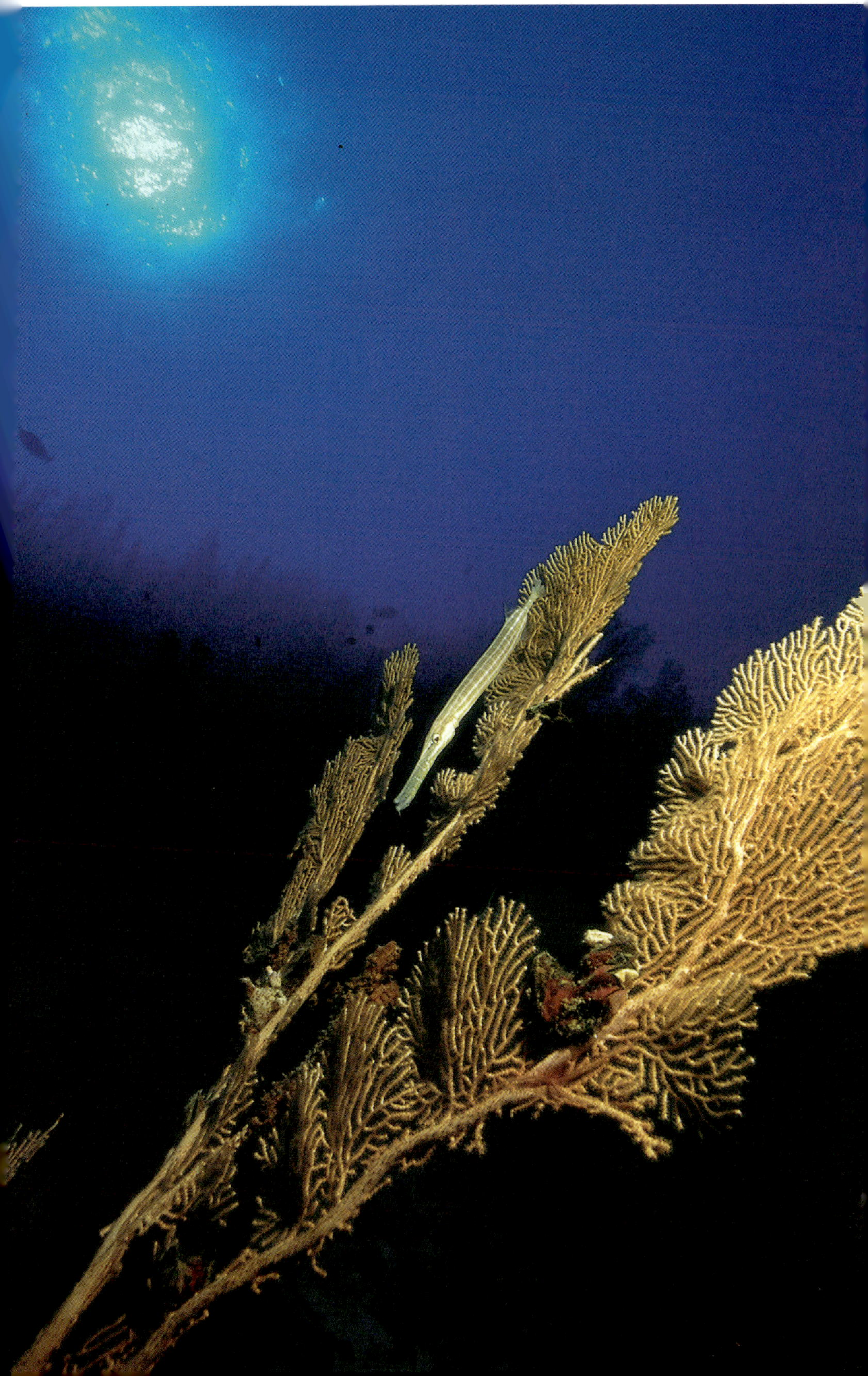

Marble Ray Point   10

Currents:	Not everywhere, but vary from strong to very little; sometimes cold around the deep point
Visibility:	Fairly steady, 60–80 ft (18–25 m)
Surge:	Medium strong to little; found mostly near wall and below rock formation
Anchorage:	None
Sea state:	Nearly always choppy

Found on the west side of the island are the steep cliffs of Punta Maria. At the base of these cliffs, two long points project out making Punta Maria look like a headless sphinx. High up, where the monster's mouth should be, a waterfall tumbles down, pounding the rocks below.

Facing the cliff, the dive site is situated on the right-hand point. Underwater, this point continues down like two giant steps leading to a deep sandy area.

The right point of Punta Maria marks the dive site of Marble Ray Point.

An eagle ray glides along the wall at the beginning of this dive.

Enter the water anywhere along the point and descend to an area of rocks and boulders at the foot of the wall. Among these boulders can be found many eels, sea urchins, and lobsters.

Follow the wall, keeping it on your right, as it steps down. Be warned that, at the tip of the last step, the current, which could be cold, is strong and difficult to swim against. Just around the corner, the current lessens. Spread out on the sand, at this point, a dozen marble rays are often seen. Their speckled black backs make the area resemble a messed-up checker board.

So far, this is one of two places on Cocos Island where marble rays rest motionless on the bottom in a group. If approached correctly, they will allow a diver to get quite close. This is an ideal spot to study their behavior and take some pictures.

Visually, at this point, depth is deceptive—what looks and "feels" like 80 ft (25 m) is really 100–130 ft (30–40 m). Perhaps the rock contours create this atmosphere. You should carefully monitor your depth on this dive.

This rock formation at Marble Ray Point resembles two cephalic fins of a giant manta ray.

Farther around the point, and up to the right, silhouetted against the turquoise-blue water, is a rock formation that looks like the two uncurled cephalic fins of a manta ray. Apart from attracting schools of snappers and other fish, these curved arms make an interesting background for photographs. However, there is a strong surge in this area that makes life a little difficult.

Apart from whitetip sharks and eagle rays, manta rays can occasionally be seen passing overhead. Sea urchins litter the area. The juveniles are distinguishable by their black-and-white ringed spines and colorful bodies.

The stepped reef walls are covered with sponge growth. White and pink fan coral is more abundant here than on other sites.

The black-and-white rings on the spikes of this sea urchin indicate it is a juvenile. ▶

50

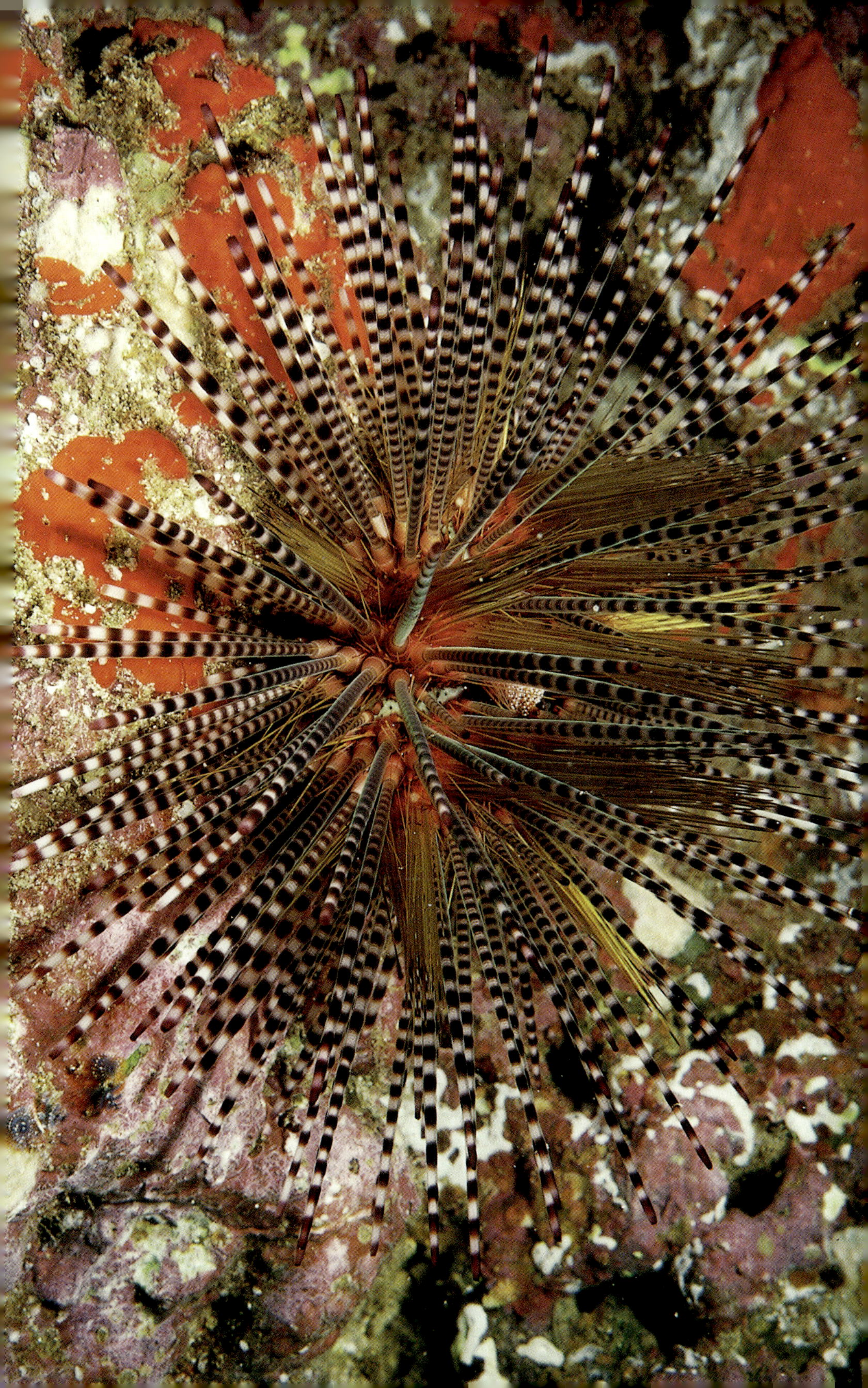

Chatham Bay   11

Current:	None to little
Visibility:	Badly affected by run-off, 60 ft (18 m) at best
Surge:	Not usually very much. But is effected by swells from the northeast
Anchorage:	One of the best
Sea state:	Usually calm, except for northeast or easterly seas

  This is by no means one of the top dive sites, but it should be mentioned. This bay is the most popular anchorage and is an alternative dive site to Manuelita East. This is also one of the bays where pirate ships would have stayed and unloaded their treasure to be buried onshore.

  A struggling coral reef covers the floor of this bay. Many factors have led to its deterioration. Probably the largest contribution is the heavy rain run-off, which deposits layers of silt onto the reef, slowly strangling it. Parrotfish and pufferfish feed on the tiny coral polyps. Hundreds of teeth

Crown-of-thorns starfish consume and destroy hard corals throughout the world and Cocos Island has not escaped their deadly behavior.

This bivalve clam filters food from the surrounding water and shuts instantly when approached.

Hawkfish can be spotted day and night on Cocos' shallow reefs.

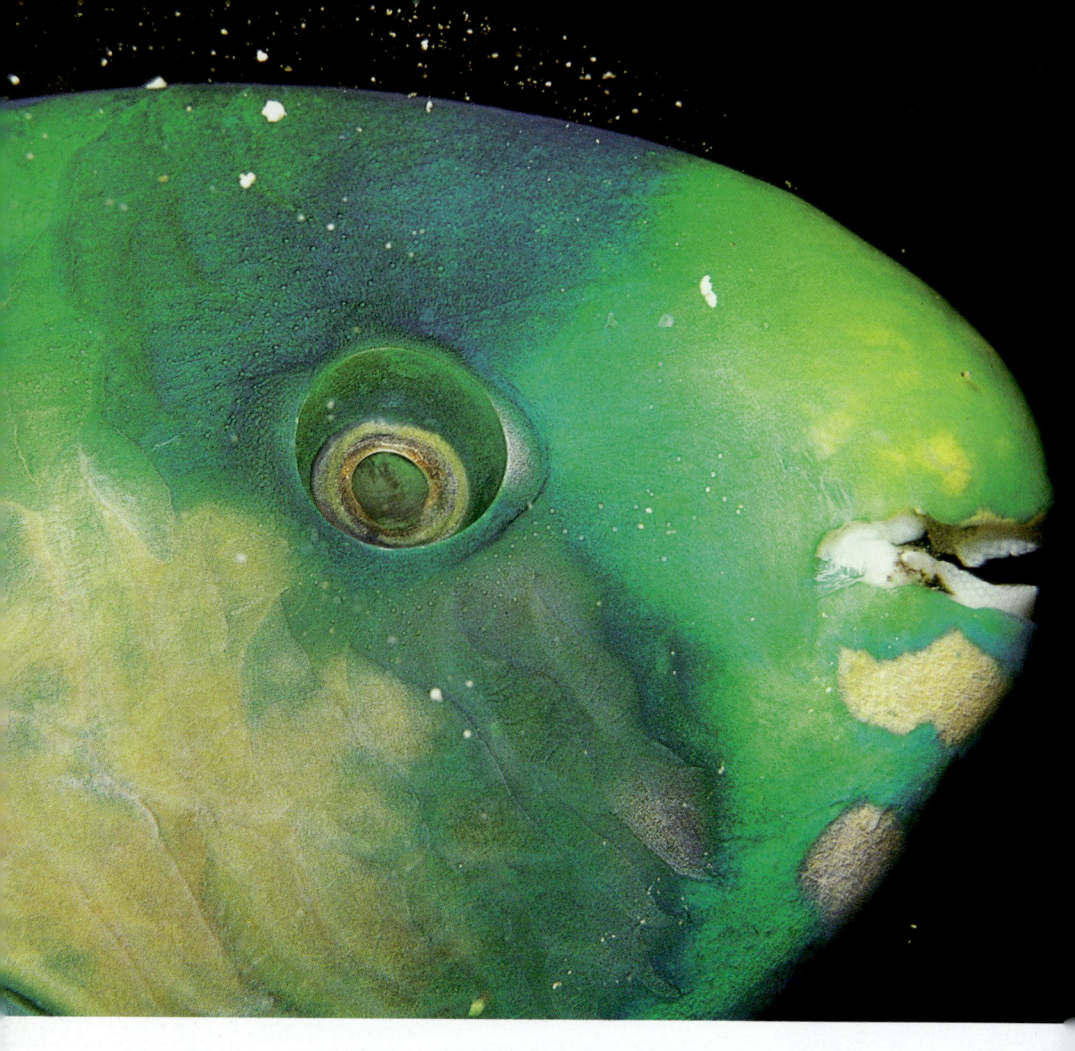

Parrotfish sleep at night and for protection cover themselves with a mucous membrane that they expel from their mouths.

It is thrilling to look up and see dozens, sometimes hundreds, of hammerheads schooling above you, especially when it's time to surface. (Photo: Robert Bryning) ▶

marks, where they have taken a mouthful, cover the reef, adding to the general worn look of the area.

During the day, butterflyfish and damselfish are a few of the fish that can be seen roaming the reef for food. This would certainly be a good snorkeling and night dive spot, where eels and many types of crustaceans emerge from under the reef to feed. Take care to avoid the black spiky sea urchins that carpet the seabed and make dives treacherous.

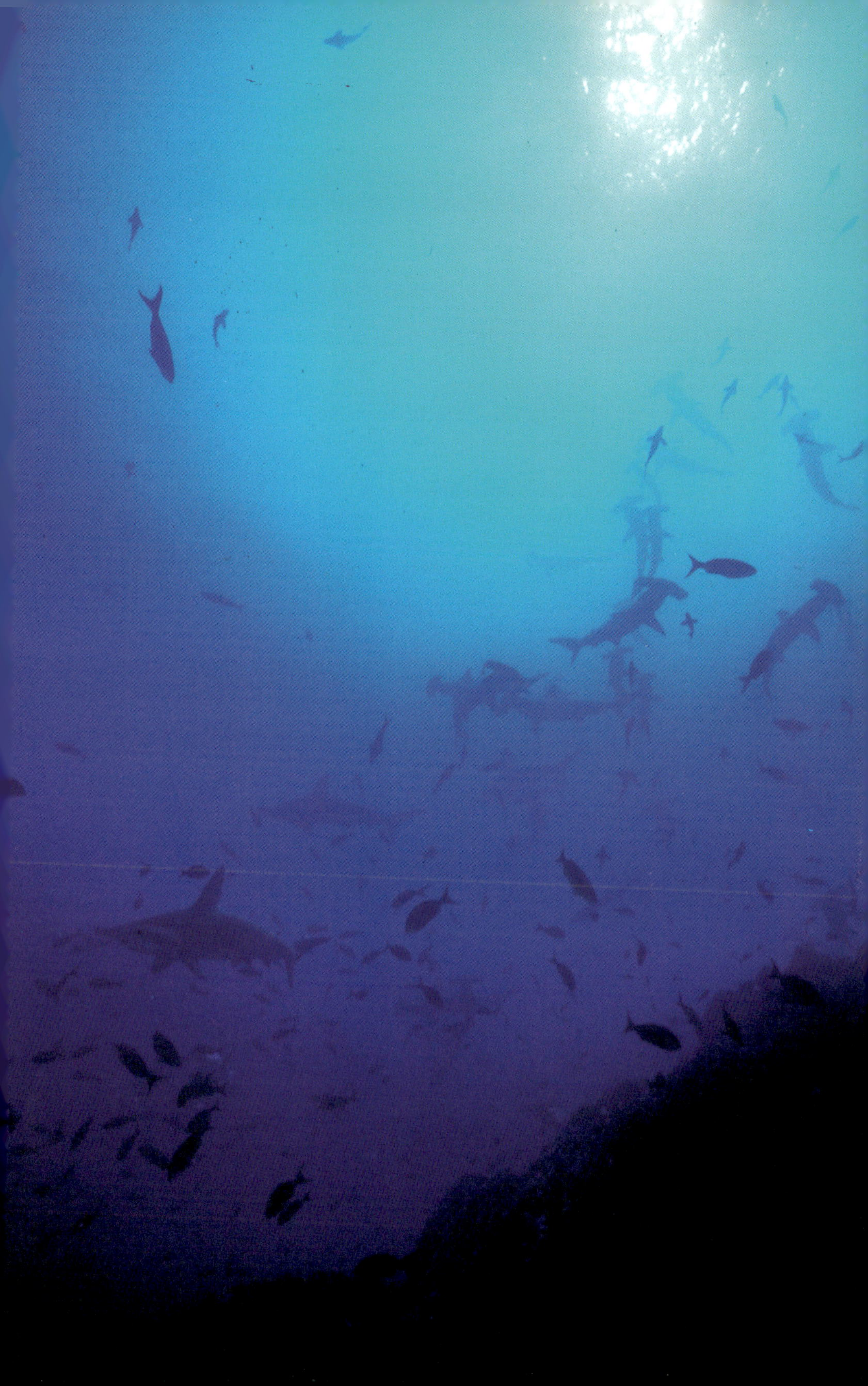

Wafer Bay   12

Current: None
Visibility: Not great
Surge: None
Anchorage: Good
Sea state: Nearly always calm, except for northerly seas

   This shallow bay has a rocky and sandy bottom. There is no reef, but the remains of two pirate ships rest on the seabed, possibly sunk under the weight of treasure?! A few fragments of scattered timber are the only remnants of the wrecks. The area has been extensively dived by treasure hunters over the years and most items of interest or value have been removed long ago.
   There is a tunnel or deep cave on the left side, set in the rock. It is visible above and below the water level, but strong surges make entry impossible.
   Reef life is sparse, although it is possible to see rays, eels, and some fish.

Until they are lit by a dive light, Pacific starfish appear to be blue/lilac instead of this pinkish color.

Porcupine pufferfish can inflate themselves as protection against predators, but try not to antagonize them.

The spectacular crescent-shaped beach at Wafer Bay is peaceful now, but it has been trampled by many a pirate's boot and could tell many a tale.

3

Safe, Smart Diving

Preparation

As mentioned, except for the park rangers' station, Cocos Island is uninhabited. Therefore, it is essential to make sure all diving and photographic equipment is checked and in working order before you leave home. There is no opportunity to buy, rent, service, or mend any equipment associated with this type of trip. If you have not dived recently, or are unsure

A tiny blenny trying unsuccessfully to look inconspicuous on a coral strand.

Yellow cup coral comes alive at night, stretching its tentacles out to catch passing food. ▶

of how you might cope with open-ocean diving, it may be wise to take a short diving refresher course at home. The dive sites are all reached with a dinghy ride; dive masks have been known to fall over-board, so take a back-up. If you use a dive computer, install fresh batteries, and stock up on batteries for all photographic equipment. Once the boat has left Puentarenas, there are no stores to buy from.

Apart from basic first-aid kits on the dive boats, there are no other medical facilities on Cocos Island. With this in mind it may be prudent to pack a few medical supplies, just in case. Antiseptic creams that reduce swelling, pain, and itching for most marine scratches and cuts are a practical inclusion; so are ear drops for use after each dive to help dry the ear and prevent infection. If earache is already felt, then a fungicidal ear-drop treatment is helpful. If this gives no relief, then use an antibiotic ear drop, which would normally need a doctor's prescription.

The nearest recompression chamber is Roatan, Honduras.

Reef Etiquette

To build the beautiful reefs we enjoy it takes hundreds, sometimes thousands of years. A boat load of careless divers can quickly start its deterioration. Given a choice, we would not want to harm any marine organism. We have a choice. Dive with alertness and caution for preservation of the reef and to avoid personal injury.

Lobsters are found on many of the dives at Cocos.

Don't touch any marine creature.

If it is absolutely necessary to hold on to regain control, make sure it is a rock or a dead piece of the reef.

In the case of a photographer who may need to kneel, look for a sandy area and beware of sea urchins.

Don't overextend your abilities. Sit out a dive if necessary. There will be less challenging dives available, but perhaps not so exciting.

Buoyancy control is the gateway to marine conservation. Having the correct amount of weight is an important factor of buoyancy control. Be correctly weighted appropriate to your wet suit and tank. This will greatly enhance your enjoyment of the dive. Cocos is warm water diving, so you may need a thinner wet suit than you are used to. If this is the case, you will need less weights. Ask the dive master/captain to help you assess the boat's tanks. They, too, affect buoyancy. Steel tanks are heavier than aluminum, and their buoyancy does not significantly change during the dive, so you will need less weight. Aluminum tanks become lighter as the quantity of air inside reduces, thus making a decompression stop at 15 ft

(5 m) very tricky if you are under-weighted. There may be a choice of tanks on the live-aboard.

Hazardous Marine Life

The sharks that frequent this area are mostly the hammerhead, silky, and whitetip sharks. All sharks are potentially dangerous. Unprovoked aggression is a factor, but rarely seen in these diving conditions. On the whole, close encounters are usually over-inquisitive sharks, not hungry ones. Around Cocos there is an abundance of their natural food supply, fish.

There is no sure way to safeguard yourself against diving with these creatures, other than not diving. It would be advisable to keep near the reef and/or other divers. Don't kick your fins in a frenzy or wave your arms around; stay calm, stay still, and don't panic. Sometimes cameras can be a good form of defense, because it seems that whenever a diver is ready to take a picture the sharks won't come near.

The tiny spike-like nematocysts of fire coral penetrate the skin and cause a burning sensation. Ordinary vinegar helps soothe the irritation.

There are about 350 species of scorpionfish around the world, and most share the common characteristics of excellent camouflage and venomous spines.

It would be fair to assume that if you have chosen to dive in Cocos Island, then shark encounters are high on the priority list, and are not something to be avoided.

On a secondary scale, when reef diving, the hazards are scorpionfish, sea urchins, and fire coral. All of these can be avoided by careful, buoyancy-

Barracuda schools are more easily approached by divers than other fish species.

controlled diving. Scorpionfish and sea urchins rest motionless on the bottom and, with a quick glance down, can be spotted if you need to come to rest on the seabed.

DAN. The Divers Alert Network (DAN) operates a 24-hour *emergency* number—(919) 684-8111. This provides divers and physicians with medical advice on treating diving injuries. DAN can also provide the latest information on the location of the nearest recompression chamber, which for Cocos Island is in Roatan, Honduras.

DAN is a non-profit membership organization. Subscription to its newsletter, which is available throughout the world, is around $15 per year. Members are able to buy a $25 medical policy that covers air ambulance, hospital treatment, and recompression chambers for diving injuries. Divers should make sure their insurance policy or holiday/vacation coverage includes diving accidents.

DAN's address is: DAN, Box 3823, Duke University Medical Center, Durham, NC 27710, USA. Their non-emergency number is (919) 684-2948.

Appendix—Diving Operations

Live-Aboards

The Undersea Hunter—90-ft (27-m) long, accommodates 14 guests in 6 cabins
The Sea Hunter—115-ft (35-m) long, accommodates 18 guests in 8 cabins.
Okeanos Aggressor—120-ft (40-m) long, accommodates 22 guests in 10 cabins.

Main booking agent for both *Hunter* boats in the U.S.A.—

See & Sea Travel Service
50 Francisco Street, Suite 205
San Francisco, CA 94133
(800 or 880) 348-9778 (toll free)
(415) 434-3400
fax: (415) 434-3409

Main booking agent for Aggressor fleet—

Aggressor Fleet, Ltd.
P.O. Drawer K
Morgan City, LA 70381
(504) 385-2628
fax: (504) 384-0817

Main booking agents for both *Hunter* boats in Europe—

Maldives Scuba Tours, Ltd.
Robert Bryning or Samantha Harwood
Diss Business Centre
Frenze Hall Lane, Diss
Norfolk IP21 4EY
England
(44) 1379-651555
fax: (44) 1379-651888

International Diving Expeditions
(800 or 880) 544-3483

Index

Boldface page numbers indicate photos.

Accommodations, 11
Anchorages, 1, 10, **14,** 52
Barracuda, 20, **63**
Belcher, Captain Edward, 11
Bonito, Benito, 13, 15
Blenny, 37, 39, **58**
Bolivar, Simon, 16
Boobie birds, 5
Book, 8
Butterflyfish, 38, 54
Caves, 3, 16, 56
Chatham Bay, 5, 8, 10, **13, 14,** 15, 35, 52
Chatham Bay (dive site), 21, 52–54
Chatham, HMS, 15
Clam, **53**
Cleaning station, 28, 39
Climate, 6, 7
Cocos
  finch, 11
  Island, **4, 5,** 6, 10, 11, 13, 14, 19, **23,** 49, 58
  map, 21
  weather, 6, 7, 22
Conservation, 11, 60
Coral, 24, 36, 38, 41, 50, 52, 58, **61,** 62
Costa Rica, 4, 11, 16
Cousteau's Sea Mount (dive site), 21, 42–43
Crabs, **41**
Crown of thorns, **52**
Dampier Head, 21, 29, 44
Dampier, William, 14
DAN, 62, 63
Darwin, 11
Davis, Edward, 11, 13, 14
Decompression, 21, 22, 26, 43, 60
Devonshire, HMS, 15
Dirty Rock (dive site), 21, **24,** 24–26
Dolphins, 20, **22**
Dos Amigos I, (dive site), **12,** 21, 31–32
Dos Amigos II (dive site), **12,** 21, 33
Eel, 6, 21, 35, 39, **40,** 42, 49, 54, 56
Endemic, 11
First-aid, 58
Fishing, 11
Flora and fauna, 10, 13
Frogfish, 6, **38,** 39
Galapagos Islands, 10
Geography, 10
Gissler, Augustus, 16
  Punta, 21, 24

Goatfish, 20, 38, **39**
Gold, 13, 15, 18
Graham, Captain Bennet, 15
Grunts, 20, 38
Hawkfish, 35, **53**
Hazardous marine life, 61
Hiking, 8
History, 12
Humbolt Current, 7
Intertropical convergence zone, 6
Iglesias,
  bay, 21, 27
  mount, 8, 11, 12, 21
Inscriptions, 10, **13,** 15
Jacks, **19,** 20, 25, 27, 29, **30,** 36, **37,** 38
Jeweled boxfish, **18,** 38
Lima treasure, 16, 19
Live-aboards, 1, 11, 23, 61
Lobsters, 21, 35, 49, **60**
Manta Ray Point (dive site), 21, 44–46
Manuelita
  Island, 21, 35
  East (dive site), 21, 38–41, 52
  West (dive site), 21, 35–37
Marble Ray Point (dive site), 21, 48–51, **48**
Marine park, 11
Marlin, 20
Mary Dear, 18, 19
Milkfish, 38
National park services, 11, 21
Night diving, 38, 41, 54
Ocean triggerfish, 39
Octopus, 28
Palmetos, 20
Park rangers, 1, 8, 11, 58
Parrotfish, 38, 52, **54**
Photography, 36, 39, 50, 59
Pinnacle, 21, 25, 27
Pirates, 13, 15, 16, 52, 56, 57
Preparation, 58
Punta Maria, 21, **48**
Puntarenas, 1, 5, 59
Pufferfish, 38, 52, **57**
Rainbow runners, 20, 25, 38, **46**
Rainfall, 7
Rainforest, 7, **8**
Rating system, 3
Rays
  devil, **7,** 20, **45**
  eagle, 20, **49,** 50

  manta, 20, 26, **44,** 46, 50
  marble, 20, 25, 26, 29, **34, 35,** 49
Recompression chamber, 12, 59, 62
Reef etiquette, 60
Safety, 3, 61
Sailfish, 20
Scorpionfish, **62**
Sea eagle, 5
Sharkfin Rock (dive site), 21, **29,** 30
Sharks
  scalloped hammerhead, **6,** 20, 24, **25,** 26, 28, 33, 35, **36,** 39, 43, 61
  silky, 20, 27, 61
  silvertip, 20, **43**
  whitetip reef, 20, 25, 27, **28,** 29, 33, 35, 36, 39, **42,** 50, 61
Sir Francis Drake, 13
Snappers, 20, 25, 26, **27, 31, 32, 33,** 35, 50
Snorkeling, 38, 54
Spanish
  cities, 14
  colonies, 12
  galleons, 12, 15, 18
Sponges, 36, 50
Squirrelfish, 35, 39
Starfish, 39, **56**
Stevenson, Robert Louis, 5, 23
Submerged Rock (dive site), 21, 27–28
Thompson, Captain, 13, 18, 19
Treasure, 12, 14–16, 18–19, 20, 23, 52, 56
Tunnel, **27,** 28
Turtle, 6, 35, 38, 39, **40,** 41
Tuna, **1,** 25, 27
Tunicates, 36
Trumpetfish, 35, **47**
Urchin, sea, 49, 50, **51,** 54, 60, 62
Vancouver, Captain George, 15
Wafer Bay, 5, 8, 10–11, 16, **17,** 57
Wafer Bay (dive site), 21, 56
  Lionel, 14
Waterfalls, **1,** 4, 5, 8, **9,** 10, 48
Weston Bay, **10,** 21, 35
Whalers, 14
Whale shark, **2,** 20, **26**
Wrecks, 56
Yachts, 10, 11, 22
Yellow cup coral, 39, **59**

65

Pisces Books®

Be sure to check out these other great books from Pisces:

Caribbean Reef Ecology
Great Reefs of the World
Skin Diver Magazine's Book of Fishes, 2nd Edition
Shooting Underwater Video: A Complete Guide to the Equipment and Techniques for Shooting, Editing, and Post-Production
Snorkeling . . . Here's How
Watching Fishes: Understanding Coral Reef Fish Behavior
Watersports Guide to Cancun

Diving and Snorkeling Guides to:

Australia: Coral Sea and Great Barrier Reef
Australia: Southeast Coast and Tasmania
The Bahamas: Family Islands and Grand Bahama
The Bahamas: Nassau and New Providence Island, 2nd Ed.
Bali
Belize
The Best Caribbean Diving
Bonaire
The British Virgin Islands
California's Central Coast
The Cayman Islands, 2nd Ed.
Cozumel, 2nd Ed.
Cuba
Curaçao
Fiji
Florida's East Coast, 2nd Ed.
The Florida Keys, 2nd Ed.
The Great Lakes
Guam and Yap
The Hawaiian Islands, 2nd Ed.
Jamaica
Northern California and the Monterey Peninsula, 2nd Ed.
The Pacific Northwest
Palau
Puerto Rico
The Red Sea
Roatan and Honduras' Bay Islands, 2nd Ed.
Scotland
St. Maarten, Saba, and St. Eustatius
Southern California, 2nd Ed.
Texas, 2nd Ed.
Truk Lagoon
The Turks and Caicos Islands
The U.S. Virgin Islands, 2nd Ed.
Vanuatu

Available from your favorite dive shop, bookstore, or directly from the publisher: Pisces Books®, a division of Gulf Publishing Company, Book Division, Dept. AD, P.O. Box 2608, Houston, Texas 77252-2608. (713) 520-4444.

Include purchase price plus $4.95 for shipping and handling. IL, NJ, PA, and TX residents add appropriate tax.